GREAT DEBATES
TOUGH QUESTIONS / SMART HISTORY

THE FIGHT FOR FREEDOM

By
Geoffrey C. Harrison
and
Thomas F. Scott

NORWOOD HOUSE PRESS

CHICAGO, ILLINOIS

Norwood House Press
PO Box 316598
Chicago, Illinois 60631

For information regarding Norwood House Press, please visit our website at:
www.norwoodhousepress.com or call 866-565-2900.

Photo Credits:
Library of Congress (4, 9, 12, 13, 15, 17, 19, 21, 22, 24, 27, 30, 34, 43, 44);
University of Chicago Library (10); Upper Case Editorial Services (11);
Minnesota Legislative Reference Library (18): The Neale Company (23); Black Book Partners (28);
Associated Press (35, 36, 38, 41); Bryn Mawr College (43).

Cover Photos: Toby Talbot/AP (left), Pat Wellenbach/AP (right).

Edited by Mark Stewart and Mike Kennedy.
Designed by Ron Jaffe.
Special thanks to Content Consultant Kim Greene.

Paperback ISBN: 978-1-60357-607-9

The Library of Congress has cataloged the original hardcover edition with the
following call number: 2013017970

Manufactured in Heshan City, Guangdong, China.
238N—012014

COVER: The fight for freedom in America started with the rights of
African Americans and women. Today it includes the gay community.

Contents

INTRODUCTION

Note: Words that are **bolded** in the text are defined in the glossary.

INTRODUCTION

We have issues ...

History doesn't just happen. It isn't made simply with the delivery of a speech or the stroke of a pen. If you look closely at every important event in the story of America, you are likely to discover deep thinking, courageous action, powerful emotion ... and great debates.

This book explores the debate over the individual rights of United States citizens. Throughout much of history, freedom and liberty came at a very high price. The American colonies fought a long, agonizing war against England to gain their independence. The result of this victory was a nation founded on principles of freedom and liberty.

The Declaration of Independence states that "all men are created equal" and that every person is born with basic human rights, including "life, liberty, and the pursuit of happiness." Unfortunately, rights proclaimed on paper sometimes do not translate into society.

As this illustration shows (left to right), Benjamin Franklin, John Adams, and Thomas Jefferson played central roles in the writing of the Declaration of Independence. The document was the first to spell out the freedoms granted to United States citizens.

Join the Debate

Debate is the art of discussing a controversial topic using logic and reason. One side takes the affirmative side of an issue and the other takes the negative side. Remember, however, that a great debate does not necessarily need to be an argument—often it is a matter of opinion, with each side supporting its viewpoint with facts. The key is to gather enough information to create a strong opinion. Out in the real world, debate has fewer rules and can get noisy and ugly. But on the big issues in America, debate is often how compromises are made and things get done.

The primary author of the Declaration of Independence was Thomas Jefferson. He was a student of the **Enlightenment**, a movement to improve society through science, tolerance, and reason. Yet Jefferson also owned more than 40 African-American slaves. They enjoyed none of the human rights to which Enlightenment thinkers thought everyone was entitled.

Women in America during colonial times were also interested in gaining more freedom. Their lives were immeasurably better than those of slaves, but they were also denied basic human rights. In most parts of America, everyday life followed the laws of the church. And in most religions in the 1700s, women were not on an equal footing with men.

Women were expected to be wives and mothers. Once married, any rights they had disappeared. In some places,

Make Your Case

In Chapter 2 through Chapter 5, you will find special sections entitled **Make Your Case**. Each one highlights different sides of the debate on individual rights using quotes from prominent Americans. **Make Your Case** lets you analyze the speaker's point of view … and challenges you to form an opinion of your own. You'll find additional famous opinion-makers on the debate in Chapter 7.

for example, women who owned property had the right to vote. They gave up that right after marriage. Most of the work done by women was unpaid. In many ways, they were treated as if they were slaves, and there was nothing they could do about it.

After America won its freedom, the founding fathers began setting the course for the new nation. The Constitution and Bill of Rights spelled out what the government could do and what new rights Americans could expect to enjoy. U.S. society at the time favored the interests of free white men who owned large amounts of property. Women, African Americans, and other minority groups had little to no say in how the country was run. For example, when the Constitution and Bill of Rights were written, neither ended slavery or granted equal rights to women. Keep this in mind as you read about these great debates.

1 Can a country based on freedom deny liberty to more than half its people?

When the Constitution was being written, the idea that women should be formally granted equality with men was not discussed. By contrast, the status of African Americans was a very hot topic. Southern leaders wanted slavery to continue unchanged and pushed to have slaves counted as part of each state's population. This would give those states a greater say in how the national government was run. Having just risked everything in the fight for freedom, many Americans debated whether this was the kind of country they had fought for ...

AFFIRMATIVE SIDE

When you start a new country, you get to make your own rules. Slavery may go against the basic principles of freedom, but without it the Southern economy might collapse and weaken the nation. For the United States to remain united, some compromises must be made.

When James Madison helped write the Constitution, he didn't believe that slavery would last.

The Three-Fifths Solution

As this debate raged, an un-comfortable compromise was eventually made. Southern states were allowed to count each slave as three-fifths of a person when cal-culating population. The goal of the founding fathers was to create a strong national government. If Southern states felt they were being **short-changed**, they might have rebelled. Some Southerners—including George Washington and James Madison, who wrote much of the Constitution— believed that slavery would slowly disappear. Indeed, part of the deal was that the international slave trade would end in 20 years. And in 1808 it did.

NEGATIVE SIDE

If we compromise on the rights and freedoms of the human beings who helped build this nation, what kind of country are we? Slavery is wrong. If part of our economy can only survive on the backs of slaves, then let that part die, and we'll deal with the consequences.

Make Your Case

"Every master of slaves is born a **petty** tyrant."

▶ *George Mason, 1787*

Mason was one of the founding fathers—and himself a slave owner. He made this statement while the Constitution was being drafted. He believed that continuing the practice of slavery made Americans no better than the English "tyrant" they had just overthrown.

In what ways did the practice of slavery weaken America?

However, the buying and selling of African Americans *within* the U.S. was still allowed. With the cotton industry growing in the South, planters saw only one way to meet the demand for labor: slaves. Over the next few decades, the Southern economy was built on the backs of African Americans. As the nation expanded westward in the 1800s, the question of whether new states would become "slave states" stirred up tremendous controversy. Some people believed that slavery violated the basic ideas upon which America was built and did not want to see the practice extended. Southerners viewed the potential **abolition** of slavery as a threat to their economy, culture, and way of life.

Make Your Case

"It is the idea of the *wrong* of slavery which has misled, and is continuing to mislead, the American mind."

▶ *T.W. Hoit, 1860*

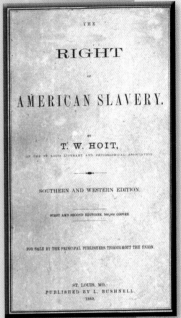

Hoit was a popular writer and lecturer in the 1850s. While admitting that slavery itself might be wrong, he did not feel that enslaving Africans was wrong. In *The Right of American Slavery* (right), Hoit claimed that Africa was a "barbaric" land, and that African Americans might not know what to do with freedom once they achieved it.

Is there ever a circumstance where slavery could be considered a good idea or ending slavery could be considered a bad one?

Women's Rights

During the first half of the 1800s, little progress was made in the area of women's rights. The country was growing, and some factory work was available to women, but these jobs were dangerous and the conditions were poor. In most cases, women were paid less than the men in the same factory. Some jobs had been open to women during the 1700s in medicine and education, but nearly all disappeared. Where women did enjoy some power and influence was in

Lucretia Mott was one of the pioneers of the women's rights movement.

the anti-slavery movement. They proved to be exceptional organizers and, in some cases, popular speakers.

In the 1840s, Elizabeth Cady Stanton and Lucretia Mott used their experience as abolitionists to campaign for women's rights. In 1848, they held a two-day convention in Seneca Falls, New York. The most significant development of that meeting was the creation of the Declaration of Rights and Sentiments, which was modeled on the Declaration of Independence. It spelled out the rights that would make women equal to men.

The most controversial part of this document was women's suffrage (the right to vote) in local, state, and national elections. Many worried that this idea was so radical that it would keep people from reading the entire

Frederick Douglass, who fought to abolish slavery, saw a great deal in common between the plight of African Americans and women.

Declaration of Rights and Sentiments. Frederick Douglass, a former slave and leader of the movement to abolish slavery, spoke at the Seneca Falls convention. He convinced the group to keep suffrage in the Declaration.

Now consider *this* ...

During the early 1800s, abolitionists began attracting a large following. However, the leaders of the movement often disagreed on strategy. Douglass believed that the Constitution was an anti-slavery document and wanted to use it to fight the practice of human bondage. William Lloyd Garrison felt the Constitution supported slavery and wanted to burn it. John Brown was unconcerned with documents. His solution was to start a bloody uprising among slaves. *If you had lived at this time, would you have challenged the legality of slavery, or would you have supported violent rebellion?*

2 Is it the government's job to fight for the freedom of one group?

By the mid-1800s, it had become clear that the United States would have to deal with this question. Slaves could not fight for themselves, and abolitionist leaders such as John Brown were willing to kill and be killed to see their bondage end. The result was uncontrolled chaos and violence throughout. In 1861, after Abraham Lincoln was elected president, the Civil War began as 13 slave states broke away from the Union and formed a separate government. As **casualties** mounted, many debated whether ending slavery was worth the high price in human lives …

AFFIRMATIVE SIDE

If one group is being denied its rights and liberties by another, then it is the government's job to correct this injustice by whatever means necessary. If a group is being denied its freedom by the government itself, then blood may have to be spilled before a solution is reached.

Issuing the Emancipation Proclamation made Abraham Lincoln a hero to African Americans nationwide.

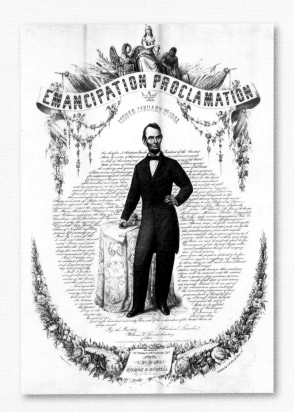

The Civil War and Reconstruction

From the start of the Civil War, slaves who lived close to the fighting tried to make their way to Union lines. Many stayed in Union camps to support the Northern troops. In 1862, President Lincoln cleared the way for African Americans to form their own **regiments**. They were sorely needed, as the number of Northern volunteers fell sharply that year.

In 1863, Lincoln issued the Emancipation Proclamation. It declared slaves in 10 Southern states to be free.

NEGATIVE SIDE

The job of government is to protect the freedoms guaranteed by the Constitution, not to fight for them. Our system of government rewards patience and persistence. It was created so that problems could be addressed through reason and discussion. Violence should never be an option for any group if the law is on its side.

As the Civil War wound down, there was some question as to the legal meaning of the Emancipation Proclamation. So in the weeks before the fighting ended in 1865, Lincoln pushed through the Thirteenth Amendment. It declared an official end to the practice of slavery. For the first time in the South, African Americans could legally marry and own property.

After the war ended, Southern states were welcomed back into the Union. Almost immediately, state governments in the South began passing legislation that limited the rights of the millions of now-free African Americans. Federal troops were sent back to the South, this time to protect the rights of former slaves. This period was known as Reconstruction. Most Southerners resented the presence of blue-coated soldiers and were unwilling to accept African Americans as equals.

Now allowed to vote and run for office, African Americans elected more than 1,500 men of color to public positions. In 1870, Hiram Revels of Mississippi was the first African American elected to the U.S. Senate. That same year, Joseph Rainey of South Carolina became the first African American to be elected to the U.S. House of Representatives. Southern states responded with laws that took the vote away from hundreds of thousands of African Americans. They also crafted **Jim Crow laws**, which **segregated** black and white society. Meanwhile, African Americans were targeted for violence by vigilante groups, such as the Ku Klux Klan.

"There never will be complete equality until women themselves help to make laws and elect lawmakers."

▶ *Susan B. Anthony, 1906*

Anthony made this statement a few weeks before she passed away. The goal of her lifelong struggle for equal rights was securing the vote for women, which would open the way for women to participate in government.

Why would some people have opposed the idea of women holding office in the 1800s?

The Fourteenth and Fifteenth Amendments

In 1868, the Fourteenth Amendment was added to the Constitution. It guaranteed equal rights under the law to all persons. Its goal was to protect the rights of former slaves. However, part of the amendment also stated that only *male* citizens would be counted in determining how many representatives each state would get in Congress. The Fifteenth Amendment, passed two years later, guaranteed voting rights regardless of a person's race, education, or

"Women shouldn't be dragged into the dirty pool of politics."

▶ *Thomas Girling, 1917*

Girling was a member of the Minnesota legislature for 20 years. He shared the view of many male politicians of his era. Among other things, he believed that women would find politics distasteful.

Is our country stronger when all groups, including women, take part in governing?

whether they had been a slave. Those rights, however, were not extended to women.

In response to these laws, Elizabeth Cady Stanton and Susan B. Anthony formed the American Woman Suffrage Association. They focused on getting individual states to allow women to vote. It was not until 1893 that the first state—Colorado—fell in line. Utah and Idaho soon followed. These Western states were desperate to attract more women. Politicians saw that giving them the vote was a powerful incentive.

In 1896, the leaders of more than 100 clubs for African-American women created the National Association of Colored Women. Among the founders of this organization were educated women of color, as well as heroic figures such as Harriet Tubman, a guide on the famous **Underground Railroad**. Their ranks soon swelled to more than a quarter-million members. In the early 1900s, this group helped make important changes in both the **civil rights** and women's rights movements. *As African Americans and women, did NACW members have an advantage or disadvantage in the fight for freedom?*

Harriet Tubman spent her life working to protect the rights of African Americans and women.

Are some Americans more equal than others?

In 1896, the United States Supreme Court heard a case known as *Plessy v. Ferguson*. It involved a man named Homer Plessy, who was arrested in New Orleans, Louisiana, for refusing to leave the "whites-only" car of a passenger train. Plessy was one-eighth African American, but by local law he was considered black. The justices decided that a state could keep races separate but equal. In other words, as long as there was a "coloreds-only" car, the Constitution had not been violated. This decision gave legal backing to the South's Jim Crow laws, creating a new debate …

AFFIRMATIVE SIDE

As long as a state provides people of color with the same public services and accommodations as white people, then the policy of separate but equal works for everyone. It helps keep order and avoid conflicts between blacks and whites.

When President Woodrow Wilson called World War I a "war for democracy," women took the opportunity to ask about their rights.

Women and the Vote

By the early 1900s, the fight for freedom had become a fight for equality on all fronts. Women's groups were starting to pressure Congress to pass a Constitutional amendment to give them the vote. The main opposition to this effort was funded by saloons and liquor manufacturers. They were afraid that when women got the vote, they would make alcohol illegal. (And they were correct!)

In 1917, America entered World War I. President Woodrow Wilson told the nation it was a "war for democracy." This gave the women's movement a wonderful opportunity.

NEGATIVE SIDE

Separate can never be equal. Will children in a school for African Americans receive the same education as children in a school for whites? Will the quality of life be the same for the two races if whites are in charge of deciding what "equal" means?

The National Women's Party took the fight right to the White House—literally. They began picketing right in front of the president's residence. No one had ever done this before. Their message was clear: *How can you send soldiers to fight for democracy and deny it to 20 million women at home?* Many of the protesters were jailed, including the group's leader, Alice Paul. President Wilson instructed Congress to start working on the Nineteenth Amendment, which said the right to vote could not be denied based on sex.

The NAACP

Equality came more slowly for African Americans. In the early 1900s, leaders from black communities began meeting to discuss strategies for improving their situation. Segregation was the rule in the South. But in most parts of America, non-whites were often treated as second-class citizens, too. In 1909, the National Association for the Advancement of Colored People (NAACP) was formed. Its early leadership included

Morefield Story, a white supporter of civil rights, was the first president of the NAACP.

"If one race be inferior to the other socially, the Constitution of the United States cannot put them upon the same plane."

► *Henry Brown, 1896*

Supreme Court Justice Brown explained the court's 7–1 decision in *Plessy v. Ferguson* by saying that it viewed the case as involving social issues, not legal ones—and supported the concept of separate but equal. Blacks and whites in Louisiana, the justices claimed, shared the same civil and political rights. Therefore, the court had no reason to strike down the state law.

Should the U.S. Supreme Court base any decision it makes on the belief that one group of people is inferior to another?

both black and white men and women, all interested in social reform. Its goals included winning political, educational, social, and economic equality, and eliminating racial hatred and discrimination.

The NAACP enjoyed tremendous success almost from the start. It built up a membership of nearly 100,000 in just

Make Your Case

"Such legislation [separate but equal] ... is inconsistent not only with that equality of rights which pertains to citizenship, national and state, but with the personal liberty enjoyed by everyone within the United States."

▶ *Marshall Harlan, 1896*

Harlan was the only Supreme Court justice to disagree with the *Plessy v. Ferguson* ruling in 1896. His courage inspired Thurgood Marshall as an NAACP lawyer.

In what ways did segregation affect the personal liberty of all U.S. citizens?

a few years. It persuaded the Supreme Court to rule that cities could not create "black" neighborhoods. It convinced President Wilson to promote African-American officers during World War I. The NAACP also pressured the police to make arrests and prosecute those responsible for race riots and lynchings.

The NAACP's investigative work influenced a 1923 Supreme Court decision that protected the rights of African-American **defendants** in trials. Another victory came in 1938, when the Supreme Court found that the University of Missouri violated the "separate but equal" ruling in *Plessy v. Ferguson*. The school denied an African-American student admission to its law school based on his race—even though there was no "equal" law school for people of color in Missouri. This ruling set the stage for the NACCP's greatest triumph, a Supreme Court decision that overturned this **double standard** once and for all.

Now consider *this* ...

For most of its first 50 years, the NAACP's main battle was to defeat the "separate but equal" decision in *Plessy v. Ferguson*. As more skilled legal minds joined the NAACP, it developed a strategy that was different from the ones used by women's groups to secure the vote. Instead of protesting and trying to embarrass the government, the NAACP fought in the courts, launching a series of lawsuits designed to give African Americans the same rights as white people. Each time the NAACP won, it was like taking a brick from the foundation of segregation. *Could the women's movement have benefitted from taking a similar legal approach to the NAACP's?*

4 Can freedom exist without equality?

In 1954, the efforts of the NAACP led to a Supreme Court case known as *Brown v. Board of Education*. It began as a **class action suit** by three African-American parents in Topeka, Kansas. On advice from NAACP leaders, they tried to enroll their children in a white school. After they were turned away, they sued the Board of Education, claiming that racial separation was unconstitutional. By the time the case reached the Supreme Court, it included four other similar cases. All claimed that the equal treatment guaranteed by the Fourteenth Amendment had been violated. The debate took a new turn ...

AFFIRMATIVE SIDE

The operation of separate schools based solely on race is harmful to African-American children. It makes them feel inferior and scars them for life. This violates the "equal protection" clause of the Fourteenth Amendment.

Thurgood Marshall's impact on the civil rights movement can still be felt today.

Brown v. Board of Education

The Supreme Court justices agreed unanimously that society had changed in the 58 years since *Plessy v. Ferguson*. Separate but equal was clearly unconstitutional. The NAACP's earlier victories—including desegregation of trade unions and the military—made it almost impossible for the court to vote otherwise. One of the architects of the NAACP's brilliant legal strategy was Thurgood Marshall. He later became the first African American appointed to the Supreme Court.

NEGATIVE SIDE

There is no evidence that segregation harms children, and therefore the Fourteenth Amendment does not apply. Some non-white schools actually may be better than white schools because they receive extra funding for Native-American children.

When Jackie Robinson broke the color barrier in Major League Baseball, he became a symbol of progress for African Americans.

After the Brown decision, the strategy of the NAACP changed. With federal law now unquestionably behind the cause, the fight for freedom took to the streets. Initially, the movement stressed mass demonstrations and peaceful protest—and these tactics were successful. However, in the late 1960s, anger and frustration boiled over in some cities, leading to deadly riots. The leaders of the civil rights movement were split on which strategy would serve them best.

Among the heroes of this era were Jackie Robinson and Martin Luther King, Jr. Robinson integrated the country's richest (and "whitest") sport, Major League Baseball. Under a relentless barrage of insults and threats, he demonstrated quiet dignity and amazing skill to become baseball's Most Valuable Player. Dr. King, a Baptist minister, rose to prominence leading a bus **boycott** in Montgomery, Alabama. The boycott began with the arrest of Rosa Parks, after she refused to give her bus seat to a white passenger. It showed the effectiveness of mass demonstration as a weapon in the fight for freedom.

"We who engage in non-violent direct action are not the creators of tension. We merely bring to the surface the hidden tension that is already alive."

▶ *Martin Luther King, Jr., 1963*

These words came from a letter written by King while in jail in Birmingham, Alabama. He was arrested for leading protests in the city and was mistreated while in custody. King's letter marked an important point in the civil rights movement.

In what ways might a strategy of non-violent protest and **civil disobedience** *bring tensions to the surface?*

The Civil Rights Act

After risking life and limb to face down the forces of segregation, the civil rights movement won the sympathy and support of most Americans. The choice to oppose the ugliness of racism with non-violence proved to be a wise one. Just a decade after *Brown v. Board of Education*, President Lyndon Johnson signed the Civil Rights Act of 1964. It outlawed discrimination against racial, ethnic, national, and religious minorities. A major part of this legislation was the desegregation of all schools. One year

Make Your Case

"Be peaceful, be courteous, obey the law, respect everyone … but if someone puts his hand on you, send him to the cemetery."

▶ *Malcolm X, 1963*

Not everyone in the Civil Rights movement preached peaceful protest. For many years, Malcolm X urged African Americans to answer violence with violence. He criticized the efforts of King and his followers. Malcolm believed in using "any means necessary" to achieve freedom, justice, and equality.

In the fight for freedom, should people use all methods at their disposal or should some be off-limits?

later, Johnson signed the Voting Rights Act of 1965. It restored the vote to millions of African Americans who had been eliminated from voter rolls by unfair laws.

The Civil Rights Act of 1964 was also a significant moment for the women's movement. The language made it clear that the same laws preventing people from discriminating against African Americans now protected women, too. Not only did this lead to progress in education and employment opportunities, it also started a frank discussion about the "reproductive rights" of women—the ability to decide when they would have children, and also when they would not. Women who had become pregnant against their wishes had only one choice: abortion. This option was dangerous (and illegal during most of the 1800s and 1900s).

Now consider *this ...*

The Civil Rights Act of 1964 offered no protection to another group of Americans whose freedoms were extremely limited. Throughout history, there have always been people who were drawn to members of their own sex—men to men, and women to women. During the 20th century, as the population became more mobile and cities grew, it was easier for a person to find others who shared their feelings or beliefs or lifestyle. In almost all societies, same-sex relationships were frowned upon, both by the law and by organized religion. This was true in America, too. **Should the rights of gay Americans be protected under the same laws that protect the rights of women and African Americans?**

Should laws protect the rights and freedoms of all Americans equally?

Starting in the 1960s, the freedoms of all Americans were being examined and discussed in new ways. State and national laws believed to be restricting the rights of any citizen in any way were held up to great scrutiny. The fight for freedom was taking place in the streets, in the courts, in the media, and sometimes right in living rooms across America. In 1973, the Supreme Court ruled that abortion was no longer illegal in the United States. This was viewed as a victory in the battle for women's rights, but it brought about an entirely new debate ...

AFFIRMATIVE SIDE

The decision to terminate a pregnancy is a personal one. Any law that prevents an adult woman from doing this violates her right to privacy. The bottom line is that no one should be "forced" to give birth.

Roe v. Wade

The separation of church and state was one of the founding principles of the U.S. But America is one of the most religious Western nations. Religious values played a very important role in legislation until the 1960s, when the Supreme Court began making the separation crystal clear. In 1973, the court's decision in *Roe v. Wade* lifted the legal ban on abortion, but left it up to individual states to regulate the practice. Almost immediately, Americans were divided into two camps.

"Pro-life" supporters wanted to make abortion as difficult as possible. "Pro-Choice" supporters wanted to make the decision as informed and unpressured as possible. The debate over abortion gave the church a new voice in politics. Although a religion could not influence legislation, its followers *could* affect the election of the people *making* the laws. That has made the abortion debate a social and political flashpoint for more than four decades.

NEGATIVE SIDE

This is about the child. The mother's rights end when she makes the decision not to protect herself from becoming pregnant. Our laws are meant to apply equally to every American, even an unborn American.

The Gay Rights Movement

The 1970s was an era of spirited protest and **activism**. The pioneering success of the African American civil rights movement in the 1950s and 1960s made standing up and fighting for your rights culturally acceptable. This provided opportunities for many political and social movements to move from the shadows into the headlines, including the gay rights movement. By the 1990s, same-sex relationships had gained great acceptance in American culture. One of the major goals of the movement was for same-sex couples to enjoy the same freedoms and benefits as other married people in America. The problem was that the federal government had never officially *defined* what marriage is (or isn't). The government simply left that up to individual states.

Make Your Case

"I love my children. I love my friends, my brother. Heck, I even love my mother-in-law. Should we call these relationships marriage, too?"

▶ *Rick Santorum, 2008*

Santorum, a presidential candidate in 2012, believed that marriage should be between a man and a woman. Many Americans share this view. They do not wish to stop people from loving each other, but oppose the legal bond of marriage for same-sex couples.

Should the government recognize same-sex marriage the same way it does marriage between men and women?

Make Your Case

"Marriage is a civil right. If you don't want gay people to marry in your church, good for you. But you can't say they can't marry in your city."

▶ *Julian Bond, 2009*

Bond, the chairman of the NAACP, was an important figure in the civil rights movement. He believed the fight for freedom reached beyond the interests of African Americans.

Was Bond smart to apply the idea of constitutional separation of church and state to same-sex marriage?

For example, prior to 1967, the government recognized mixed-race marriages in states only where they were legal. But would the federal government recognize a same-sex marriage that was declared legal by a state? This was an important question. "Married status" granted basic rights that other married couples had, and would give same-sex spouses tremendous financial benefits, too. In 1996, the

The rainbow-colored flag has become a symbol of the gay rights movement.

question was answered with passage of the Defense of Marriage Act (DOMA). It defined marriage as being between a man and a woman—and was a bitter setback for the gay rights movement.

In the years that followed, the gay rights fight continued. Several states legalized same-sex marriage or civil unions. (Civil unions are meant to provide the same benefits, protections, and responsibilities as marriage.) Because of DOMA, however, the federal government did not extend the benefits beyond state borders. Some states chose to recognize same-sex marriages in other states, while refusing to marry same-sex couples in their own state. The result was confusion, frustration, and a lot of same-sex couples wondering whether they were actually married or not. In 2012, President Barack Obama announced that he supported same-sex marriage, opposed DOMA, and hoped lawmakers would support the concept of marriage equality.

Now consider *this* ...

The gains made by the African American civil rights movement in the 1960s included a government policy known as Affirmative Action. It grew out of a federal law that prevented job discrimination based on color, religion, sex, or national origin. Affirmative Action involved programs that tried to fix years of imbalance by creating opportunities in the workplace and in education specifically for minorities, and in many cases women as well. Some complained that this was "reverse discrimination," but the courts upheld Affirmative Action policies time and again. However, in 2012 and 2013, the Supreme Court agreed to hear a challenge to Affirmative Action. *After more than 50 years, has Affirmative Action evened the odds, or will ending this policy bring a return to discrimination in education and the workplace?*

6 Find your voice

For many, the issue of equal pay is the next great hurdle in the women's rights debate.

I n recent years, three issues have been at the center of the fight for freedom. These are complicated questions that invite many points of view. Much like other issues in this debate, they involve economics, politics, powerful fears, and strong emotions. There is a very good chance that people will be debating these issues throughout your lifetime.

Should different people be paid different wages to do the same job?

This has been a key point of the women's rights movement. The Fourteenth Amendment guarantees equal treatment to all Americans, yet many companies are guilty of offering female employees less than male employees for similar work. In a 2006 Supreme Court case, it was revealed that women were paid on average 80 cents for every dollar that men make for the same job. Based on this case, Congress passed a law in 2009 that gave women more legal options to fight wage discrimination. The next fight in this battle may involve immigrant workers. Like women, they are routinely paid less than others doing the same work.

Is it worth giving up some of our freedom to be safer?

This question has been debated for more than a century, but it is more important today than ever. Our government is not allowed to spy on its citizens or search their property without establishing first that they pose a threat to society. The right to privacy is fiercely protected in America.

In decades past, law enforcement agencies have sought permission to monitor phone conversations of people suspected of posing a threat to society. This helps the government stop major crimes, such as acts of terror, before they happen. Today, those wishing to do harm to the U.S. are more likely to use email and texting to communicate. They have taken advantage of new technologies, partly because they know the government is limited in how it can track this type of communication. In 2013, the Federal Bureau of Investigation (FBI) asked to change the law to allow agents to "tap" these conversations as they happen. This power might help prevent a terrorist attack in the final hours or minutes before it occurs. It might also mean the government could look in on anyone's texts and emails.

Should there be limits to the freedoms of the disabled?

In 1990, Congress passed the Americans with Disabilities Act. The new law said that public buildings, schools, and workplaces had to be accessible to people in wheelchairs. In 2008, the law was amended to accommodate people with other disabilities—including physical and mental handicaps—that limit someone's ability to participate in everyday activities. In many cases, making these changes was complicated and expensive. Today, some people question what would happen if the government's official definition of "disabled" expanded further. For example, might the Americans with Disabilities Act one day include conditions such as obesity? If so, what would the impact be?

President Barack Obama meets people who have benefitted from the Americans with Disabilities Act on the 25th anniversary of the legislation.

All the issues in this chapter are being discussed as part of the national debate on individual rights. Will we ever reach a "middle ground" on these questions? Now is the time to join the national conversation. Think about these issues and consider both sides of these debates. Where do you stand? One day soon—through the candidates you support, the dollars you spend, and your own personal feelings about church and state—you will have a voice!

7 Point — Counterpoint

The debate on individual rights has been greatly influenced by public opinion over the years. That opinion is shaped by many factors, including personal experience, common sense, and what others write or have to say. We think about the different sides of an issue. We look at how it affects us, our family members, and our friends. We consider the best solutions. And we weigh what the smartest and most influential people believe.

This was true in the 1700s and 1800s, when Americans got their information from pamphlets, newspapers, and speeches. It was true in the 1900s, when radio and television brought ideas to an even wider audience. It remains true today, as we scan websites, blogs, and social media. The voices in this chapter have helped shape the debate on the fight for freedom. The words may be a little different, but the passion behind them would fit in any era …

"Women have won the right to higher education and economic independence. The right to become citizens of the state is the next and inevitable consequence of education and work outside the home." *M. Carey Thomas (right), 1911* ◀

"Woman suffrage has brought no social, legal, or industrial **betterment** to women, or to the state, while it has brought social and domestic **discord**." ▶ *Helen Kendrick Johnson, 1909*

Thomas was the president of Bryn Mawr College and a leader in the fight for the vote. She was convinced the gains made by women in academics and the workplace would soon guarantee them a say in government. Johnson was the leading woman in the fight *against* women's suffrage. She believed that ladies of wealth and privilege already had great influence on American politics through their husbands. Opening the vote to all women would reduce that power. Johnson used Colorado to "prove" her point—women had won the vote there 16 years earlier and the state had not been transformed in any obvious way.

How might the growing number of well-educated or working women have made it more likely that they would win the vote?

"To separate them from others of similar age and qualifications solely because of their race generates a feeling of inferiority as to their status in the community that may affect their hearts and minds in a way unlikely ever to be undone."

Earl Warren, 1954 ◀

"We shall get a finer, better balance of spirit; an infinitely more capable and rounded personality by putting children in schools where they are wanted, and where they are happy and inspired, than in thrusting them into hells where they are ridiculed and hated."

▶ *W.E.B. DuBois (left), 1935*

DuBois was a college professor, author, and founding member of the NAACP. Few people were more respected in the early days of the civil rights movement. In the 1930s, he questioned how desegregation of schools would work. His comments were later used to defend segregation in the *Brown v. Board of Education* case. In his opinion on this case, Supreme Court Justice Warren concluded that keeping schools segregated would do far more harm than good.

What kind of long-term damage did segregated schools do to society as a whole?

Point — Counterpoint

"There are some forty thousand children in California …
who live with same-sex parents, and they want their
parents to have full recognition." *Anthony Kennedy, 2013* ◀

"The debate over same-sex marriage is not over
tolerance. It is about the purpose of the institution
of marriage." ▶ *Mitt Romney, 2006*

Romney was Governor of Massachusetts in 2006. He agreed
with the view that the purpose of marriage was to create
children. During a Supreme Court debate about a same-sex
marriage law in California, Justice Kennedy pointed out that
sometimes another purpose of marriage is to *raise* children.

Is the issue of same-sex marriage something that should be decided by the courts?

There has never been a better time to make your voice heard. No matter which side of an issue you take, remember that a debate doesn't have to be an argument. If you enjoy proving your point, join your school's debate team. If your school doesn't have one, find a teacher who will serve as coach and get more students involved. If you want to make a real splash, email the people who represent you in government. If they don't listen now, they may hear from you later … in the voting booth!

GLOSSARY

Abolition — The movement to end slavery in the United States.

Activism — The use of energetic campaigning to bring about social change.

Betterment — The process of improving something.

Boycott — A refusal to do business with a company.

Casualties — People killed or injured in a war or accident.

Civil Disobedience — The refusal to comply with certain laws as a means of peaceful protest.

Civil Rights — The rights of citizens to freedom and equality.

Class Action Suit — A lawsuit brought by a small group of people on behalf of a much larger group.

Defendants — People who are on trial for a crime.

Discord — Disagreement between people.

Double Standard — A rule or law that is applied unfairly to two different groups.

Enlightenment — A movement starting in the late 1600s that favored reason and individual thought rather than tradition.

Jim Crow Laws — State and local laws that created two sets of public facilities—one for whites and another for blacks—including public schools, transportation, restaurants, restrooms, and water fountains.

Petty — Small or unimportant.

Regiments — Units in the military, usually led by a colonel.

Segregated — Divided based on race.

Short-Changed — Not given what was due.

Underground Railroad —A secret network that helped slaves escape.

SOURCES

The authors relied on many different sources for their information. Listed below are some of their primary sources:

Women's World: A Timeline of Women in History. Irene M. Franck & David M. Brownstone. HarperPerennial, New York, 1995.

The American Women's Almanac. Louise Bernikow. The Berkley Publishing Group, New York, 1997.

Century of Struggle: The Women's Rights Movement in the United States. Eleanor Flexner & Ellen Fitzpatrick. The Belknap Press, Cambridge, MA, 1996.

African American Biographies. Walter L. Hawkins. McFarland & Co., Jefferson, NC, 1992.

Voices of Freedom: An Oral History of the Civil Rights Movement from the 1950s through the 1980s. Henry Hampton & Steve Fayer. Bantam Books, New York, 1991.

RESOURCES

For more information on the subjects covered in this book, consider starting with these books and websites:

The Gay Rights Movement. Jennifer Smith. Greenhaven Press, Farmington Hills, MI, 2003.

The Origins of the Women's Movement. LeeAnne Gelletty. Mason Crest, Broomall, PA, 2013.

The Civil Rights Movement. Lydia D. Bjornlund. Reference Point Press. San Diego, CA, 2013.

BlackPast.Org
www.blackpast.org

The Equal Rights Amendment: Unfinished Business for the Constitution
http://www.equalrightsamendment.org/

Civil Rights Timeline
http://www.infoplease.com/spot/civilrightstimeline1.html

Women's Rights Timeline
http://www.infoplease.com/spot/womenstimeline1.html

Gay Rights Timeline
ttp://www.infoplease.com/ipa/A0761909.htm

INDEX

Page numbers in **bold** refer to illustrations.

AUTHORS

GEOFFREY C. HARRISON and **THOMAS F. SCOTT** are educators at the Rumson
Country Day School, a K thru 8 school in Rumson, New Jersey. Mr. Harrison is the head
of the math department and coordinator of the school's forensics team. Mr. Scott has
been teaching upper school history at RCDS for more than 25 years and is head of that
department. They enjoy nothing more than a great debate … just ask their students!